# HELP IS ON THE WAY FOR:

# Study Habits

Written by Marilyn Berry
Pictures by Bartholomew

CHILDRENS PRESS ™

CHICAGO

Childrens Press
School and Library Edition

Copyright ©1985 by Marilyn Berry
Institute of Living Skills, Fallbrook, CA
All rights reserved.
Printed in the United States of America.
**ISBN 0-516-03237-2**

Executive Producers: Ron Berry and Joy Berry
Producer: Ellen Klarberg
Editors: Nancy Cochran and Susan Motycka
Consultants: Kathleen McBride, Maureen Dryden, and Donna Fisher
Design: Abigail Johnston
Typesetting: Curt Chelin

Is **studying** getting you down?

Hang on! Help is on the way!

If you have a hard time

- finding the right study tools,
- finding time to study, and
- dealing with study problems...

...you are not alone!

Just in case you're wondering...

...why don't we start at the beginning?

# What is Studying?

When you use your mind to learn about something, you are studying. There are many ways you can study. Here are a few examples:

• You can study by reading.

• You can study by practicing.

• You can study by investigating.

• You can study by memorizing.

# Why Do You Study?

There is much information that you will need to know throughout your life. For the most part, you will learn this information by studying. Here are some examples:

• Math

• Geography

- Reading

- Science

# Studying and School

It would be very difficult to learn everything you need to know on your own. That is why you go to school. Schools provide teachers and materials to help you learn. *You* provide the time and effort for studying. How much you learn depends mostly on you.

Studying does not have to be boring or hard work. In fact, learning can be fun and exciting. You can take the boredom and some of the work out of studying. The key is to get organized. All it takes are three simple steps.

# Three Steps to Getting Organized

## STEP ONE
## ORGANIZING YOUR STUDY ENVIRONMENT

To get the most out of your study time, you need a good study environment. This includes having a proper place to study and having the necessary tools on hand. Without these basic ingredients, studying can be a disaster.

## Finding a Place to Study

If possible, it is best to choose one special place that can be set aside as *your* permanent study area. If you have a space that you do not have to share with others, you can set up your area and keep it ready for your study time. You might set up your study area in

- your own room,
- your own corner, if you share a room, or
- a place in your house that is seldom used by others.

If you cannot find a permanent study area, don't get discouraged. There are other places you can go. You might try to find a place in your house that can be reserved for your study time. The public library is also a very good place to study.

Ask your parents or guardians to help you. Maybe they can come up with some creative ideas.

No matter where you choose to study, your study area should be neat and orderly. It is also important that your study area

- is a quiet place without distractions,
- has proper lighting,
- is the proper temperature (not too hot or cold),
- has a large work space such as a desk or table, and
- has a comfortable, straight-backed chair.

## Gathering the Proper Tools

You can make your studying easier, and you will save time, by keeping the proper study tools on hand. These study tools should include study supplies and resource books.

**Important Study Supplies.** There are some supplies that should be included among your study tools at all times. Here is a list of those supplies:

lead pencils
pencil sharpener
erasers
colored pencils, pens, or crayons
ink pens (black and blue)
paper clips
rubber bands
ruler
note book paper (lined and unlined)
construction paper
note cards
scissors
scotch tape
glue or paste
note book
calendar

**Extra Study Supplies.** There are some additional supplies that are helpful but not necessary. You never know when they might come in handy!

paper punch, brads
stapler and staples
compass, protractor
Scratch paper
graph paper, tag board
Covers for reports
file folders
Plastic container
to hold supplies
boxes for
storing papers

**Important Resource Books.** There are a few resource books that can help you a great deal with your studying. These books are available in junior editions and in paperback form. Learning how to use these books and keeping them handy will make studying easier:

- dictionary
- atlas
- thesaurus
- grammar book

**Extra Resource Books.** Encyclopedias will play an important part in your studying. If you do not have a set of encyclopedias in your home, you can always find them in the library. Here are some other books that can be helpful for special assignments:

- a rhyming dictionary
- a book of synonyms and antonyms
- various idea books for major subject areas

**A Portable Study Kit.** If you do not have a permanent place to study, or if you choose to study in different places, you may want to put together a portable study kit. This kit should include samples of your study supplies and the reference books you use most often. These things can be stored in a small box or pack and will be ready to go anywhere you want to study.

Setting up a good study environment takes time. You might need to make it a long-term project. You can start with the most important items and add to your collection a little at a time. Here are some ideas to keep in mind:

- Keep a list of the items you need.
- Ask for a few of the items for birthday and holiday gifts.
- Ask to do extra chores to earn money, especially for study items.
- Remember to replace study items as you use them.

## STEP TWO
## ORGANIZING YOUR STUDY TIME

You may feel as though there is not enough time to do everything you want to do *and* study. Most likely, the real problem is that you do not plan your time or use it wisely. If you organize your time, you will find that there is plenty of time for both studying and recreation.

Before you can organize your study time, you need to find out how you are presently spending your time. You need to keep track of everything you do for a whole week. This will help you determine

- **when** you have time available for studying, and
- **how** much time is available for studying.

## Making a Time Chart

An easy way to keep track of your time is to make a time chart.

- Draw two columns on a piece of paper.
- At the top of one column, write "Time."
- At the top of the other column, write "Activities."
- In the "Time" column, list every hour of the day.
- In the "Activities" column, write down everything you did during each hour of the day.
- Make a time chart for every day of the week.
- Try to be as accurate as possible. The more detailed your time chart, the better.

# TiME CHART
## FOR MONDAY, SEPT. 6

| TiME | ACTiViTY |
|------|----------|
| 6-7am | Dressed for school, watched TV. |
| 7-8 | Ate breakfast, walked to school |
| 8-9 | Math |
| 9-10 | Reading |
| 10-11 | Recess, spelling |
| 11-12 | History |
| 12-1pm | Lunch |
| 1-2 | Gym |
| 2-3 | Free period - drew cartoons |
| 3-4 | Music lessons, stopped by the mall |
| 4-5 | Chores |
| 5-6 | Ate dinner, talked on phone |
| 6-7 | Did homework, talked on phone |
| 7-8 | Watched TV |
| 8-9 | Watched TV, dressed for bed |
| 9-10 | Sleep |
| 10-11 | Sleep |
| 11-12 | Sleep |
| 12-1am | Sleep |
| 1-2 | Sleep |
| 2-3 | Sleep |
| 3-4 | Sleep |
| 4-5 | Sleep |
| 5-6 | Sleep |

VERY INTERESTING.

### Studying Your Time Charts

After you have completed your time charts, you need to take a close look at them. You will find some interesting information. For now, be concerned with your free time. Free time is any time in which you choose your own activities.

- Add up all your free time for the week.
- Determine how much of that time was used for studying.
- Determine how much of the time was used for other activities.

As you study your time charts, you may find that
- you have more free time than you thought,
- you don't spend as much time studying as you thought, and
- you spend too much time on other activities.

Don't get discouraged. With a little planning, you can learn to get your studying done and still have time to spare.

### Reserving Your Study Time

Look at your time charts one more time. See if there are regular times that can be set aside for studying. If you reserve a block of time each day, you will always be sure to have time available for studying.

## Using Your Study Time Wisely

There are several things you can do to get the most out of your study time:

- Look over the assignments you need to complete. Make a schedule for your time.
- Get right to work.
- Do your hardest assignments first.
- Take a short break between assignments.
- Complete all assignments due the next day.
- If possible, see that you are not disturbed.

# STEP THREE
## MAKING YOUR STUDY PLAN

Your studying will be more meaningful if you have a study plan. This includes
- setting goals for yourself, and
- discovering your own learning style.

## Setting Your Goals

To set your study goals, you need to ask yourself an important question: "What do I want to achieve with my studying?" It might be to get a certain grade. It might be to improve in every class. Your goals will determine how you spend much of your study time, so think carefully when setting your goals.

Here are some things to keep in mind as you set your study goals:

- Be realistic. Don't set goals that are out of reach.
- Don't waste your time setting goals that take little or no effort to achieve.
- List your goals in order of importance. This will remind you which goals need the most attention.

### Discovering Your Own Learning Style

There are different ways that people learn. How a person learns can affect the way he or she studies. Here are some examples:

**Visual learners** learn best by using their sight. They spend most of their time reading and rereading their study material. They also learn by looking at charts and illustrations.

**Audio learners** learn best by using their hearing. They like to have information explained to them. Their study time is more meaningful when they read their study material aloud. Some find that using a tape recorder is helpful.

**Active learners** learn best by doing. When studying, they find it helpful to make their own charts, graphs, and illustrations. They also use any practice material available.

Think about how you like to learn.

- Do you like to learn by reading on your own?
- Do you like to have someone explain information to you?
- Do you like to practice what you have learned?

You may learn by using more than one learning style. The important thing is to study the way that is best for you.

# Dealing With Study Problems

There might be times during the school year when you have problems with your studying. Perhaps you are falling behind in your work. Maybe you do not understand some of the material that is being taught.

One way to tell if you are having study problems is by your grades. The purpose of grades is to tell you whether or not you have learned the things you were supposed to learn. If you get a low grade on a test or in a class, you are probably having study problems.

## Getting Help

When you are having study problems, there's no need to panic. There are several places you can go to get help.

**Teachers.** Perhaps the best resources for help are your teachers. They know exactly what you are studying and where you could be having problems. If you ask them, they will help you.

**Students.** Sometimes another student can help you with your study problems. Choose a classmate who is doing well in your class and ask for help. Sometimes, other students can explain things as well as the teacher.

**Professional Tutors.** A professional tutor is someone who teaches privately. If your parents or guardians think you need help on a regular basis, they can hire a professional tutor. This type of help gives you one-on-one attention until you can get caught up in your classes.

**Summer School and After-School Programs.** Many schools offer programs after school and during the summer for students who need extra help. If you are having study problems, ask at your school office if there are any of these programs available.

**On Your Own.** Sometimes, study problems can be handled by putting in a little extra time. You might do some extra reading at the library. You can also find extra practice materials at book stores, toy stores, and school supply stores.

## Procrastination

One of the biggest study problems that almost every student faces is procrastination. This means putting off until later what you should do now. You can overcome this problem if you remember these things:

**Getting started** is half the battle. When you have studying to do, start as soon as you can. Once you have started, the rest will seem easier.

**Bite-size pieces** are easier to swallow than one big lump. Break your work up into small portions, and study one portion at a time. This is especially important when you are working on big projects, such as written reports or studying for a test.

**Reward yourself** for a job well done. It will give you something to work toward. You might want to set up a reward for each individual task you finish. It will break up your study time and make studying more fun.

# WARNING!

If you do the things in this book studying will become easier and...

...you might even enjoy it!

**THE END**

**About the Author**

Marilyn Berry has a master's degree in education with a specialization in reading. She is on staff as a producer and creator of supplementary materials at the Institute of Living Skills. Marilyn is a published author of books and composer of music for children. She is the mother of two sons, John and Brent.